LIVING WITH
EPILEPSY

WITHDRAWN

LIVING WITH HEALTH CHALLENGES

LIVING WITH EPILEPSY

by Sara Cohen Christopherson

Content Consultant
Carl E. Stafstrom, MD, PhD, Chief, Section of Pediatric
Neurology, University of Wisconsin–Madison

LIVING WITH HEALTH CHALLENGES

CREDITS

Published by ABDO Publishing Company, PO Box 398166, Minneapolis, MN 55439. Copyright © 2012 by Abdo Consulting Group, Inc. International copyrights reserved in all countries. No part of this book may be reproduced in any form without written permission from the publisher. The Essential Library™ is a trademark and logo of ABDO Publishing Company.

Printed in the United States of America,
North Mankato, Minnesota
102011
012012

 THIS BOOK CONTAINS AT LEAST 10% RECYCLED MATERIALS.

Editor: Lisa Owings
Copy Editor: Karen Latchana Kenney
Series design and cover production: Becky Daum
Interior production: Kazuko Collins

Library of Congress Cataloging-in-Publication Data
Christopherson, Sara Cohen.
  Living with epilepsy / by Sara Cohen Christopherson.
      p. cm. -- (Living with health challenges)
  Includes bibliographical references.
  ISBN 978-1-61783-127-0
  1. Epilepsy--Juvenile literature. I. Title.
  RC372.2.C47 2012
  616.85'3--dc23
                                    2011033155

TABLE OF CONTENTS

EXPERT ADVICE

I know it can be difficult to live with epilepsy, especially as a teen. I have been working with children and teens with epilepsy for more than 25 years. I am currently chief of Pediatric Neurology at the University of Wisconsin–Madison, and I have also held positions at Harvard, Duke, and Tufts Universities.

You may feel that you don't fit in. Perhaps you feel left out of some of the activities your friends are doing, such as driving or playing certain sports. You may worry that epilepsy will keep you from being successful in college or in your career. However, you can do many things to help loosen epilepsy's grip on your life.

Take care of yourself. Clean, healthy living goes a long way toward reducing your risk of having a seizure. Make sure you get proper nutrition by eating a variety of healthy foods and taking dietary supplements if needed. Stay away from alcohol and drugs, and get as much sleep as you can.

Don't forget to take your meds. Missing a dose of your prescribed medication is a sure way to bring on a seizure. Develop ways to remind yourself to take your meds.

Protect yourself. Even minor head injuries or concussions can make your epilepsy symptoms worse. Wear a helmet when bicycling, skiing, or engaging in other potentially risky activities.

The most important thing you can do is to never give up hope. You can live a full and relatively independent life despite your disease. Many people with epilepsy actively participate in and excel at sports, politics, and the arts. Numerous college scholarships are also available to students with epilepsy. Don't let epilepsy keep you from living up to your potential. Be safe, be smart, and live your life.

—*Carl E. Stafstrom, MD, PhD, Chief,*
Section of Pediatric Neurology, University of
Wisconsin–Madison

SOMETHING'S GOING ON: SYMPTOMS AND DEFINITIONS

L ily yawned. *Not nearly enough sleep last night,* she thought as she moved through the crowded entryway to the school building. That was when it started. She heard loud ringing noises. It almost always started like this. Fear crept over her, and she anxiously

Having a seizure at school can be scary. You'll feel safer if your friends know how to help.

looked around for someone she recognized. She knew she didn't have very long. Then she lost consciousness.

Lily's friend Jamal told her the rest of the story. He saw her right as she blacked out. She sat down on the floor and stared straight ahead. That lasted for about a minute, and then her whole body started shaking. Jamal put his jacket under her head and rolled her gently onto her side. The shaking didn't last long—just a few minutes. Then her muscles relaxed.

Lily started to regain consciousness. She was looking straight at Jamal, but it didn't seem like she recognized him. After a few more minutes, Lily sat up and rubbed her eyes. She was getting back to normal now. She groaned— she knew exactly what had just happened and was thankful Jamal was with her.

Jamal and Lily have known each other forever. He remembers the first time she had a seizure at school. They were in second grade. All the kids were watching, and everyone was curious. After it happened, Lily didn't want to go back to school and face everyone.

Now, Lily is used to having epilepsy—well, at least sort of. She still hates having seizures. It's particularly hard when they happen in public, and especially in school. She takes medication to help control her seizures. She knows what she can do—in addition to the medication—to help prevent seizures, but it can be difficult. Last night, for example, she knows she should have gotten more sleep.

But if Lily has a seizure, she now knows what to expect. Her friends all know the deal and are cool about it. Like Jamal, they know what to do if it happens. If other people see her, well, whatever. If anyone has a problem with it, Lily thinks they can just—well, you know what.

LIFE WITH EPILEPSY

Like many people with epilepsy, Lily's first seizure occurred in childhood. In fact, a first seizure typically occurs before age two. And for Lily, like for most people who have epileptic seizures, there was no obvious reason why it all started.

Not everyone has a first seizure in childhood. It's possible to have a first seizure at your age, or at any age. Some people may have epilepsy and not realize what is causing their symptoms. Not all seizures involve convulsions, or shaking, like Lily's. In fact, most seizures do not involve full-body convulsions. Some seizures make a person space out. Others cause a person to do something he or she doesn't have control over or even realize is occurring—such as hand-wringing, for example. The brain is

Not all seizures are obvious to others.

a complex organ, and the disruptions that occur with epilepsy can have a wide range of symptoms.

If you have epilepsy, you probably know it by now. But even if you know you have epilepsy, you can't possibly know everything about it. It's really a fascinating and mind-boggling condition.

THE BASICS: WHAT IS EPILEPSY?

Let's start with the basics. Epilepsy is a condition defined by periodic spontaneous seizures. In other words, to be considered to have epilepsy, you must have more than just one seizure. And the seizures must happen on their own, not because of drugs or fever.

Since epilepsy is defined in terms of seizures, it is necessary to define *seizure* too. A seizure occurs when brain activity runs offtrack. The brain is the control center of the nervous system. It is made up of hundreds of millions of nerve cells, called neurons. All your thoughts and movements are

A SEIZURE, BUT NOT EPILEPSY

Everyone who has epilepsy has had a seizure, but not everyone who has had a seizure has epilepsy. Many people experience a single seizure at some point in their lives. These seizures often have an identifiable cause. For example, head injuries, drug use, exposure to certain chemicals, and high fevers can induce a seizure. In other cases, however, a solitary seizure may have no recognizable cause. Either way, a person is not diagnosed with epilepsy until two or more seizures have occurred.

the result of electric signals sent from neuron to neuron, communicating everything your body does and experiences.

Mostly, these electric signals run smoothly through the brain. For people with epilepsy, however, part of the brain may suddenly become overactive, sending irregular electric discharges. These unexpected and abnormal signals may affect part or all of the brain. Depending on which parts of the brain are affected, the resulting seizures may take many forms. No two people with epilepsy will have exactly the same experience during a seizure. Between seizures, otherwise healthy people can lead regular lives.

THE TELLTALE SIGNS

An epileptic seizure can take many forms. Some seizures are more obvious to an observer than others. The more noticeable ones cause repetitive movements, stiffening or relaxing of muscles, or falling to the ground. Other seizures may cause a loss of consciousness so subtle and brief that people around you might not even notice. Seizures can cause feelings, smells, and even hallucinations. If you have any questions or concerns about the symptoms you are experiencing, be sure to tell a parent, school nurse, doctor, or other responsible adult who can help you get tested or treated.

HOW SEIZURES AFFECT THE BRAIN

It's not fully understood whether seizures have lasting effects on brain function. Because seizures can be different for everyone, it is impossible to say how seizures in general affect the brain. Brain damage has to do, at least in part, with the strength and frequency of the seizures. There is evidence that some seizures—particularly prolonged seizures—can cause lasting brain damage. The emergency medical condition called status epilepticus (SE) is a seizure that lasts for at least 30 minutes. It can also be a series of brief seizures that happen one after another with little or no pause in between.

THE BRAIN 101

Your brain is part of your nervous system and is the control center of your body. Different parts of your brain specialize in controlling different functions, such as sight, emotion, digestion, or the movement of your big toe. The left side of the brain controls the right side of the body, and the right side of the brain controls the left side of the body.

Neurons interact with each other continuously, sending and receiving information in the form of chemical and electric signals. Structures called dendrites branch out from one end of the nerve cell. Dendrites receive signals from other neurons. The signal moves through the axon, a tail-like part of the nerve cell, and reaches the other end, called the axon terminal. Here, the signal is sent on to another neuron.

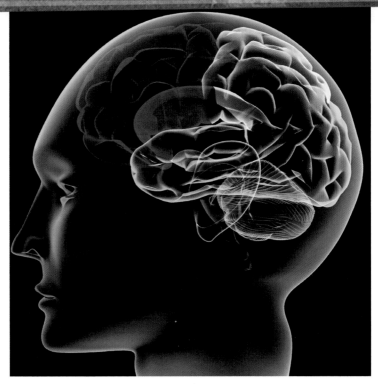

Different types of seizures affect the brain in different ways. Most seizures do not cause brain damage.

Many people with epilepsy experience memory difficulty. A number of other brain-related conditions, including depression and migraines, also occur more frequently in people with epilepsy than in the general public. It's not clear, however, whether epilepsy causes these conditions. It is very possible that the same brain issue that causes epilepsy also causes the accompanying condition.

If you have relatively short or infrequent seizures, you know that when they are over, you return to normal. If you've lost consciousness, it can take a while to feel completely alert again. But when the seizure is over, it's over.

Seizures vary in length and severity. Some seizures cause a loss of consciousness.

In general, short, infrequent seizures do not permanently or significantly damage the brain. Think of what happens when you lose reception on a cell phone. The call may break up for a little while. You might even have to hang up and redial. But when reception returns, the call goes back to normal. Losing reception can interfere with a phone call, but it certainly doesn't damage the phone. It's the same thing with most seizures. The seizure may be a short, small interference or a larger, more intense interference, but it doesn't damage the brain.

WILL THIS LAST FOREVER?

It can be frustrating not to have a solid answer, but there's no way to know for sure what will happen in any particular case, for any particular person. What we do know, however, are probabilities based on collected data about many thousands of people.

EPILEPSY BY THE NUMBERS

- Many experts estimate that between 0.5 percent and 2 percent of people will develop epilepsy at some point in their lives.[3]
- For more than half of people newly diagnosed with epilepsy, there is no known cause for the condition.[4]
- As of 2011, approximately 3 million people in the United States were living with epilepsy.[5]
- Almost 60 million people around the world have epilepsy.[6]

Most kinds of seizures can be controlled with medication. Approximately 70 percent of people with epilepsy will experience significant improvement with medication.[1] Almost 75 percent of people who have been on medication and free from seizures for several years can eventually stop medication without seizures returning.[2]

With or without seizures, people with epilepsy can live full lives. Sure, there are some challenges you have to deal with, but you are still in control of your life.

ASK YOURSELF THIS

- *If you have epilepsy, when did you find out? What was it like the first time you had a seizure?*

- *Do you know anyone else with epilepsy? What was it like to meet this person, and what did this person tell you about her or his experiences?*

- *What questions do you have about epilepsy? Where or how do you think you could find the answers to these questions?*

- *Does anything about epilepsy make you feel afraid or embarrassed? What family members or friends would you feel comfortable talking to about these fears and anxieties? Name at least two.*

- *How do you experience seizures? How do you feel before, during, and after a seizure?*

People with epilepsy can still have fun with their friends and do the activities they love.

2

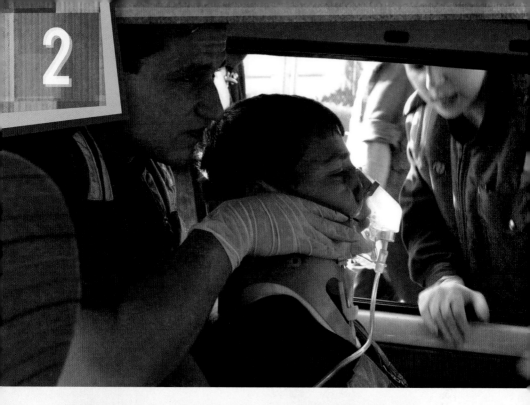

WHY ME? CAUSES, RISK FACTORS, AND PREVENTION

Kareem was in a car accident when he was 15. He was in the passenger seat. He knew he should have been wearing a seat belt, but, well, he wasn't. Kareem's friend Eric was driving. The accident wasn't Eric's fault——the other car totally blew the stop sign

A traumatic head injury can cause epilepsy.

and came crashing into them. Kareem was thrown forward, and he hit his head hard on the dashboard. He lost consciousness.

Paramedics performed first aid in the ambulance and made sure Kareem was in stable condition. At the hospital, doctors conducted a variety of tests to determine the extent of damage in Kareem's brain. They monitored him closely because his brain was bleeding.

Almost a week after the accident, Kareem had a seizure. The seizures continued, but eventually the doctors prescribed a medication that kept them under control. Kareem's doctor explained that the trauma to his brain caused some permanent changes in the way his brain worked. These changes left Kareem's brain more susceptible to seizures.

Kareem is back at school and back to a regular life, mostly. He and Eric have started a school club to promote seat belt use. They learned their lesson the hard way and hope they can spread the word about seat belt safety. Kareem still gets a sick feeling in his stomach if he thinks about the accident, and sometimes he wonders why this had to happen to him. Other times, however, Kareem feels

Epilepsy can interfere with your life, but it is manageable with the help of a doctor.

extreme happiness and thankfulness—a new appreciation for life!

THE DEVELOPMENT OF EPILEPSY

In some circumstances, the cause of epilepsy is clear. But in the majority of cases, the reason is unknown. Researchers and physicians know a lot about how neurons work, how the brain works, and how different chemical, environmental, and genetic factors affect the brain. We can measure and describe seizures in great detail. But in most cases, we don't really know *why* epilepsy develops.

Head injury is the known cause accounting for most new diagnoses of epilepsy in young adults. Brain infection, such as encephalitis or meningitis, can also leave a person at higher risk for developing epilepsy. Genetic factors certainly play a role, though not in all cases. Several known genes make the brain more susceptible to seizures. Having a stroke is a big risk factor for the development of epilepsy, but strokes are very rare in young adults. Abnormal brain structure, brain damage before birth, brain tumors, the use of certain drugs, and other factors are also known to increase the risk of developing epilepsy. Although we can name individual factors, the reality is that the development of epilepsy results from a complex combination of factors. In most cases, the cause of epilepsy is uncertain and there may be no risk factor whatsoever.

AFTER THE FIRST SEIZURE

If you've had just one seizure, you probably haven't been diagnosed with epilepsy. Although approximately 10 percent of people in the United States will have a seizure at some point in their lives, only between 0.5 and 2 percent will be diagnosed with epilepsy.[1] Of the people who develop epilepsy, the second seizure usually happens within six months of the first seizure. The vast majority of people with epilepsy have their second seizure within two years of their first seizure. If you've had one seizure, talk with your family and your doctor. The unknown can be scary, and it's important to make sure your questions and concerns are addressed.

RISK FACTORS FOR SEIZURE OCCURRENCE

If you have already been diagnosed with epilepsy, certain factors can increase your risk of having seizures. Many of the following risk factors are under your control, though some may be challenging to manage.

- Having nutritional deficiencies. You get nutrients from the food you eat. All the cells in your body use these nutrients to function. Like sleep, nutrition affects nearly every aspect of a person's life. Just like with sleep, it is important for everyone to have good nutrition, not just people with epilepsy. But for people with epilepsy, nutritional deficiencies can increase the risk of seizures.

- Interfering with medication. The main way a person can interfere with medication is by not taking it. Missing a dose of your seizure medication will, not surprisingly, increase your risk of having a seizure. But even if you take your medication on schedule, its effectiveness can

ENCEPHALITIS AND MENINGITIS

Encephalitis and meningitis are infections of the brain, most often caused by a virus or bacteria. These infections cause swelling in the brain, which can result in a headache or fever. In severe cases, encephalitis or meningitis can cause seizures, brain damage, or even death.

be compromised if you are taking other medications or if you don't take your medication at the same time every day. It is important to check with your doctor or pharmacist if you miss a dose or have questions about taking your medication.

- Being stressed out. Let's face it—it's impossible to deal with the demands of school, home life, work, and extracurricular activities, not to mention friends and family, without at least a little bit of stress! A little stress is just a fact of life, but extreme stress can be detrimental to your well-being, whether you have epilepsy or not. However, for people with epilepsy, excessive stress carries the added risk of increasing the chance of a seizure. If you think you need help de-stressing, talk with a health-care professional or other trusted adult. There are many techniques and strategies that can help you manage your stress, and you can surely find a few that work for you.

SEIZURES AND YOUR PERIOD

Some women find they are more likely to have a seizure during menstrual periods. Hormonal changes can make a seizure more likely to happen. If you find that your seizures correlate with your period, your doctor may be able to adjust your seizure medication during your period. Alternatively, you might be able to use medication to keep the hormonal changes under control.

Getting enough sleep at night is especially important for people with epilepsy.

- Not getting enough sleep. If you are like most teenagers, you don't get nearly enough sleep. According to sleep specialists, teens need approximately nine hours of sleep each night.[2] Sleep affects almost everything in a person's life and is a critical part of brain well-being. This is true for all people, not just people with epilepsy. But for people with epilepsy, not getting enough sleep can have extra risks and consequences because it makes the brain more susceptible to seizures.

- Being sick. Getting sick can put a person at higher risk for having a seizure. Of course, you can't just choose to never get sick. Still, making healthy lifestyle decisions, such as getting enough sleep, eating plenty of vegetables, fruits, and whole grains, and being active, can help keep your immune system strong and ready to fight off illness.

- Using drugs or alcohol. The illegal or recreational use of drugs can make the brain more susceptible to seizures. This one's pretty straight up: don't risk it! But if you or someone you know is struggling with drug or alcohol use or abuse in addition to epilepsy, talk to a health-care professional or an adult you trust to help get the situation under control.

NOCTURNAL SEIZURES

Getting enough sleep is never easy as a teenager, but it can be particularly challenging if you have nocturnal seizures, or seizures that happen at night. Not only can nocturnal seizures disturb your much-needed sleep, but they can also be dangerous. Those around you may be asleep and not realize you need help. If you experience nocturnal seizures, be careful to remember to take your antiseizure medication. Make sure there are no sharp objects near your bed. If it's not possible to sleep with someone close by, consider using baby monitors so a loved one can hear if you are having a seizure.

Exercise is a great way to stay healthy and relieve stress.

PREVENTION

You can't prevent epilepsy. But if you have epilepsy, there are many ways to prevent or minimize seizures. Medication is often the best way to do this. Other factors can also help keep you at low risk for seizure activity. Look back at the risk factors you just read about. Are there any areas you can improve on? If so, that's where you can focus your prevention efforts.

ASK YOURSELF THIS

- *Which risk factor for epilepsy is or would be most difficult for you to control in your life?*

- *What single lifestyle change could you make to reduce your risk factors for a seizure?*

- *Did reading this chapter change any of your ideas about why epilepsy occurs? If so, explain what you used to think and what you think now.*

- *How do you minimize your risk of seizures? What methods have you used that aren't discussed in this book? What methods mentioned in this book have you not yet tried?*

- *What area of your life do your seizures affect most? What do you feel you can't do because of your epilepsy?*

IS EPILEPSY DEADLY?

Epilepsy itself is not deadly, but people with epilepsy have a slightly greater risk of premature death than the general public. To keep this in perspective, however, this calculation includes people whose epilepsy is due to severe brain damage, stroke, and other serious conditions. For healthy individuals who just happen to have epilepsy, it's really not a worry.

SOLVING THE MYSTERY: DIAGNOSIS

S tacey started having seizures when she was 14 or 15, a freshman in high school. But it took a while before she was diagnosed with epilepsy. At first, she was told she was fainting because of stress. The first time Stacey "fainted," she was in English class. She felt tired, and her head felt heavy, so she put her head down on her desk—just for a second. The next thing she remembers is hearing a classmate shout and trying to open her eyes. Then she realized she was on the floor.

Stacey had no idea why she was on the floor, and she didn't know where she was. She was scared and confused. When she was finally able to open her eyes, she saw a man standing over her. He was talking to her, asking her questions, and it took her a while to recognize that he was the vice principal. Stacey remembers trying hard to answer him but not being able to speak. She felt like her body was submerged in molasses. After what seemed like forever, Stacey was able to answer him. Was she okay? Well, yes, she guessed she was . . . but she was still very confused about what had happened, kind of embarrassed, and pretty scared.

The vice principal and the school nurse lifted Stacey into a wheelchair and wheeled her to the nurse's office. As they rolled down the hallway, Stacey realized her body was really sore. Later, she found out she had bumped into the desks around her as she fell. She had also hit her head on the floor.

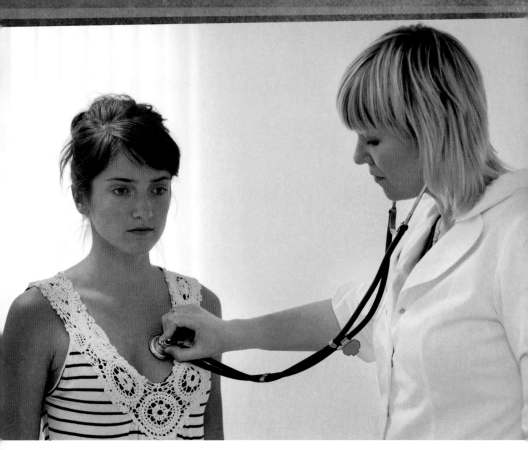

A patient must have had at least two seizures to be diagnosed with epilepsy.

Stacey waited in the nurse's office for her dad to pick her up. He took her straight to the hospital. At the hospital, the doctor checked her out. At this point, the event wasn't diagnosed as a seizure. Even for a doctor, diagnosing a seizure is hard because a seizure rarely happens at the doctor's office. After the whole ordeal, Stacey felt okay, but she was afraid it would happen again.[1]

YOUR EVALUATION

An initial diagnosis of epilepsy requires that the doctor be certain seizures have occurred. Fainting and muscular tics are often confused with seizures. When diagnosis occurs at a very young age, it can be hard to tell exactly what is going on when something abnormal happens. Your doctor will want to rule out all other possible explanations before concluding that a seizure occurred. An epilepsy diagnosis can only be made after two confirmed seizures.

Epilepsy is not a single diagnosis. There are actually many types of epilepsy, or epileptic syndromes. After you've been diagnosed with epilepsy, your doctor will want to find out what type of epilepsy you have. This depends on when and how your epilepsy began, how it has progressed over the years, what

PREPARING FOR YOUR APPOINTMENT

An epilepsy diagnosis primarily relies on a detailed description of a patient's seizures. To give your doctor a complete picture of your situation, come prepared to your appointment. Keep a record of each seizure you have, including information such as the date and time your seizure occurred, how long it lasted, and what may have triggered it. Make a list of every medication you are taking. Have a friend or family member come with you to your appointment to help you answer questions and remember information.

diagnostic tests reveal, and what type or types of seizures you have.

EEGs, MRIs, AND CTs

Diagnostic tests help doctors learn more about what is happening inside your brain. If you've been diagnosed with epilepsy, you've probably had an electroencephalogram (EEG). An EEG measures electric activity in the brain via electrodes attached to your head. The EEG detects electric activity in different parts of the brain and produces an image of the patterns, represented by wavy lines. Your doctor will interpret these patterns as either normal or abnormal. For many people with epilepsy, EEG patterns look perfectly normal. An epilepsy diagnosis does not depend on an abnormal EEG, but if the EEG is abnormal, it can help to confirm the diagnosis of epilepsy. If the EEG shows

NEUROLOGISTS AND EPILEPTOLOGISTS

Your regular physician may be well equipped to help you control your epilepsy. If your regular physician does not treat epilepsy, or if your physician refers you to another doctor, you might see a general neurologist. A neurologist is a doctor who specializes in conditions and disorders that affect the nervous system. People with seizures that are difficult to control may consult with an epilepsy specialist. An epileptologist is a neurologist who specializes in epilepsy.

abnormal activity in a certain part of the brain, it can help to identify the part of the brain in which seizure activity starts. This is an important clue that can be used to determine what treatment would be most effective.

Other tests can produce images of the brain itself. These neuroimaging tests include magnetic resonance imaging (MRI) and computed tomography (CT). The MRI machine is a long, enclosed tube. You have to lie inside the tube for the test, and it can be a little uncomfortable because it is such a small space. The scan is painless but noisy. An MRI uses a strong magnet. The magnetic field interacts with the atoms that make up your body. The MRI machine detects changes in the atoms and uses this information to produce an image of the brain. This image can help your doctor see whether abnormalities in the structure of your brain could be causing your seizures.

A CT scan is basically an X-ray of your brain. It is typically done in the emergency room. Even

TAKE A VIDEO

You may have lost consciousness and not remember the whole story about your seizures. Often, the description of a seizure relies on information from other people. If you have frequent seizures, you can try to get a friend or family member to record your seizure. Bring the recording with you to the doctor's office so your doctor can see firsthand what is happening.

if your CT scan looks normal, you will probably also have an MRI later. Both CT scans and MRIs show scars, tumors, structural abnormalities, and other clues that can be used to better understand your brain and your epilepsy.

TYPES OF EPILEPSY

There are many different epilepsy syndromes. Too many, in fact, to describe all of them here! When a person is diagnosed with epilepsy, the doctor will use all information available to try to identify the seizure type and classify the epilepsy as a particular epilepsy syndrome. It is important to identify the syndrome, because different types of epilepsy respond to different treatments. A doctor will be able to select the treatment options that are most effective for a particular syndrome.

WATCHING AND WAITING

If your doctor determines that you had a seizure, he or she will not typically recommend treatment right away. Your doctor will most likely suggest watching and waiting. This means you return to your regular life. If you are already making safe, responsible, and healthy choices, you don't need to do anything differently. A doctor may make recommendations such as not swimming alone or other common sense suggestions—things you probably do anyway. Most people who have a single seizure will not have another. If you do have another seizure, it will probably occur within six months. If two years pass without another seizure, it is unlikely that you will ever have another seizure.

The most common epilepsy syndrome in adolescents is benign childhood epilepsy with centrotemporal spikes, also called rolandic epilepsy. It is called childhood epilepsy because it starts when a person is between two and 13 years old. The average age of onset is seven years old. Centrotemporal spikes refer to the pattern on the EEG image. Approximately 95 percent of the young people diagnosed with this syndrome will completely grow out of it by the time they are 14 years old.[2]

The second most common epilepsy syndrome in children and teens is absence epilepsy. People with absence epilepsy have absence seizures, which usually begin between ages five and ten and often continue through the teenage years. A person having an absence seizure loses awareness for a few seconds. During this time, the person appears to be staring into space. Absence seizures can be dangerous if a person is driving, swimming, biking, or doing other activities in which a

HYPERVENTILATE, PLEASE

Your doctor may make you hyperventilate to try to induce a seizure. An absence seizure can often be induced when a person hyperventilates. Don't worry; it's not dangerous. If a seizure can be made to occur, it will give your doctor a chance to directly observe what is happening.

Teens with epilepsy can still lead full, normal lives.

person could be hurt if consciousness is lost. Most cases of absence epilepsy can be controlled with medication.

One of the most common epilepsy syndromes with unknown cause is called juvenile myoclonic epilepsy. It usually starts when a person is between 12 and 18 years old. Several types of seizures can occur with this syndrome. These seizures can usually be controlled with medication. Juvenile myoclonic epilepsy usually doesn't go away; it requires ongoing treatment. A myoclonic seizure causes muscles to jerk. Even if you don't have myoclonic epilepsy, you may have experienced myoclonic movement if you've ever had a full-body twitch or jerk as you were falling asleep.

ASK YOURSELF THIS

- *If you have been diagnosed with epilepsy, what was your diagnosis experience like? (Ask a parent or guardian if you were too young to remember.)*

- *If you have had to watch and wait for a second seizure, how did you feel during that time? If not, how do you think you would feel?*

- *Do you get nervous before or during a visit to the doctor? Why or why not?*

- *What would you tell your doctor about your seizures? If you lost consciousness during your seizures, whom do you trust to tell you what happened?*

- *Have you ever had someone record a video of you while you were having a seizure? If not, how would you feel about it? If so, what did you learn from watching it?*

4

THE NITTY-GRITTY: TYPES OF SEIZURES

Nico has two kinds of seizures. During one type of seizure, Nico basically spaces out. It's like someone hit the pause button on his consciousness. He makes a chewing motion with his mouth, but that's about it. The seizure only lasts for five seconds or so.

Teens with epilepsy can still play sports, but it is important to let coaches and teammates know what to do when you have a seizure.

When the seizures first started, no one knew what was going on—not even Nico. The seizures tended to happen during soccer practice. They also happened during games. That was the worst. Nico's coaches were frustrated—they thought he wasn't paying attention or that he was letting himself get distracted. In fact, Nico was briefly losing consciousness. He snapped right back into play once he came to, but a lot can happen in a few seconds on the soccer field. Nico is a really good player, but his game was totally thrown off when these pauses happened while he was playing.

The other kind of seizure usually happens soon after Nico wakes up. It's like his arms just decide to do their own thing and jerk up all of a sudden. It's a pain, because if he's holding anything it's pretty much guaranteed to end up on the floor. This type of seizure also happened for a long time before anyone figured out what was going on. Nico's sister would make fun of him and his mom would yell at him for dropping things. Nico felt horrible because he never meant to do it. When it happened, it surprised him as much as it surprised anyone else. Thankfully, these seizures almost never happened later in the day or evening. They pretty much only happened at home, first thing in the morning.

THE INTERNATIONAL CLASSIFICATION OF EPILEPTIC SEIZURES

Diagnosing epilepsy involves identifying the type of seizure that is occurring. But there are many different types of seizures. To help provide a

WHAT TO DO WHEN A PERSON HAS A SEIZURE

1. Chill out. It's important to stay calm. Remember that the seizure will pass. Tell other people to be calm. Reassure them that it's okay. Check quickly for a medical ID bracelet.
2. Look at a clock or a watch. Make note of the time. Be prepared to time the length of the seizure. (It will probably last only a few minutes.)
3. Make sure the coast is clear. Move away things that could harm the person, such as sharp objects or furniture with corners. Put something soft (a sweatshirt or blanket, for example) around the person's head to provide a sort of bumper.
4. Gently roll the person onto her or his side. This is just a precaution. If the person had something in her or his mouth, this action reduces the risk of choking. Don't try to hold the person down or put anything in his or her mouth, though.
5. Stick around until the seizure is over, and then wait until the person is alert again. Remember that after certain types of seizures, a person will be confused and disoriented. It can take a little time before the person is fully conscious again.
6. Be supportive. It can be a bummer to have a seizure. But it's nice to regain consciousness surrounded by awesome people.

common language for describing seizures, a classification system was developed in 1981. Any seizure may be classified according to the International Classification of Epileptic Seizures.

This system divides seizures into two main groups: partial seizures and generalized seizures. A partial seizure begins in a particular part of the brain. A generalized seizure affects the entire brain. Some seizures can start as partial seizures and then spread to become generalized.

WAS IT REALLY A SEIZURE?

Many symptoms seem like seizures but are actually not. Examples are fainting, rage attacks, panic attacks, tics, dizziness attacks, sleep disorders, and even migraines. Some people have spells that look like an epileptic seizure but are actually caused by stress. Sometimes these spells are called "pseudoseizures." By taking a careful history and investigating your symptoms with an EEG or other tests, your doctor will determine whether your symptoms are caused by epilepsy.

PARTIAL SEIZURES

There are three main categories of partial seizures: simple partial seizures, complex partial seizures, and partial seizures that secondarily generalize.

Partial seizures are more common than generalized seizures. A partial seizure can begin in any part of the brain.

The defining feature of a simple partial seizure is that a person does not lose awareness. This type of seizure can cause a change in muscle activity or a change in any of the senses. Partial seizures can also cause changes in body functions you don't usually control, such as your heartbeat or your digestive processes. The type of seizure that occurs depends on where the seizure activity begins in the brain. If the seizure activity starts in a part of the brain that controls movement of the toes, then the seizure will express itself as toe movements. If the seizure activity starts in a part of the brain that controls emotions, then the seizure will express itself as a feeling.

A complex partial seizure occurs when a person loses consciousness during the seizure. Most people who have complex partial seizures will experience automatisms, which are movements or activities the person does not control. This may be a repetitive movement of the hands or mouth. It could be many other things, too, such as walking, making facial expressions, or saying things out loud. After having a complex partial seizure, a person

NO, YOU CAN'T SWALLOW YOUR TONGUE

Swallowing your tongue is just not possible, even during a seizure. Take a look in your mouth. Notice that your tongue is firmly attached to your lower jaw. So, the bottom line is that it can't be swallowed.

This also means there is no need to put anything into a person's mouth while he or she is having a seizure to prevent the person from swallowing his or her tongue. Putting something in a person's mouth while that person is having a seizure is a bad idea and should never be done. It can cause damage to the person's mouth and teeth.

is confused and doesn't remember what happened. It can take a little while to get back to feeling totally alert again.

Some complex partial seizures start as simple partial seizures. The seizure then spreads to other parts of the brain, typically resulting in a type of generalized seizure called a tonic-clonic seizure.

GENERALIZED SEIZURES

There are six main categories of generalized seizures: absence, atonic, tonic, clonic, tonic-clonic, and myoclonic.

An absence seizure starts and ends abruptly. It's sort of like spacing out for a few seconds. A person may have many absence seizures each day. During the seizures, the person isn't aware of what's going on, so he or she may miss little bits of what is happening. Absence seizures are sometimes called petit mal seizures. *Petit mal* is French for "little bad."

Atonic seizures are relatively rare and cause muscles in the body to suddenly and briefly go limp. If the seizure affects leg muscles or other central support muscles, the person may fall down.

Tonic seizures cause body muscles to tighten. This tightening of the muscles can cause a person to fall. Like atonic seizures, tonic seizures are usually very short, lasting an average of ten seconds.[1] Atonic and tonic seizures mainly occur in people with severe neurological disabilities.

Clonic seizures usually occur in infants and very young children. These seizures cause rhythmic muscle jerks.

Combine the tonic with the clonic and you have a tonic-clonic seizure. These seizures start with a stiffening of the body and then move into rhythmic muscle jerks. Someone having a tonic-clonic seizure may lose bladder control.

Myoclonic seizures involve a quick muscle jerk, similar to how you might jump if someone startled you. Myoclonic seizures are more common in people with neurological disabilities.

STATUS EPILEPTICUS

Status epilepticus is a really long seizure. It can also be a series of brief seizures that happen without any pause in between. As a precaution, a seizure that lasts longer than five minutes should be treated as status epilepticus. Other types of seizures can also persist for longer than five minutes or happen in succession. If you are near someone who is having a seizure, check the time when the seizure starts. No matter what type of seizure it is, if it lasts longer than five minutes, someone needs to call 911. Seizures that last longer than 30 minutes can cause permanent brain damage.

An aura can act as a warning before a seizure,
giving you a chance to sit down in a safe place.

AURAS

Some people have a particular sensation, called an aura, before the onset of a seizure. The specifics of a person's aura can give information about where in the brain the seizure activity starts. It is important to tell your doctor what you experience if you have auras before your seizures. There are just as many types of auras as there are types of seizures. An aura might be a feeling, a movement, a vocalization— pretty much anything. You might think your aura is weird, but you should still tell your doctor about it.

For some people, an aura may come far enough in advance of the seizure that the person can prepare. If you have auras before seizures, use that alert to tell others you are about to have a seizure, to sit down, or even to get yourself to a location where the seizure can take place in relative comfort and safety. If you have simple partial seizures, the aura itself is your seizure.

ASK YOURSELF THIS

- *If you have epilepsy, what type of seizures do you have? What is your typical seizure experience?*

- *Now that you've read more about the different types of seizures, look back at Nico's story. What type of seizures do you think Nico was having on the soccer field? Why do you think that?*

- *What type of seizures do you think Nico was having at home in the mornings? Explain.*

- *Do you have auras before your seizures? If so, what do you do to prepare for your seizure?*

- *Have you ever had a seizure during school? What type of seizure was it? What was the experience like?*

5

MEDICINE AND BEYOND: TREATMENT

W hen Luis was diagnosed with epilepsy, his doctor started him on antiseizure medication. After taking the medication for almost five days, Luis noticed he had a rash all over his belly. He looked in the mirror and saw that it was on his back, too.

Epilepsy medication can cause unwanted side effects including nausea, headaches, rashes, and drowsiness.

He told his grandmother and she called the doctor's office. The nurse told her that Luis should stop taking the medicine and come into the doctor's office immediately. The doctor prescribed another medication. This time, the medication made Luis feel nauseous. He couldn't eat and was throwing up. He went back to the doctor.

Now, Luis is trying yet another medication. His doctor told him to not get his hopes up too much. He said, "Some people have reactions to medications and not everyone is able to control seizures with medication." But the doctor also said it wasn't time to give up yet. Luis had allergic reactions to the medications themselves, so he didn't even really have a chance to see whether the medications worked to control his seizures. Luis really hopes that this time he won't have a reaction to the medication. That's step one. If he doesn't have a reaction, he has hope the medication will work to control his seizures. There's only one way to find out.

CONTROLLING SEIZURES WITH MEDICATION

Almost half of all people with epilepsy stop having seizures after starting their first antiseizure medication (also called anticonvulsants or antiepileptic drugs).[1] Approximately 20 percent of people with epilepsy won't have their seizures controlled by the first medication they try, but will eventually stop having seizures after working with their doctor to find a different antiseizure medication that works.[2] It may take some time, but there's a good chance you and your doctor can find a dosage and a medication that works for you.

WHICH ANTISEIZURE MEDICATION WORKS BEST?

No single antiseizure medication is hands-down better than the others. Each medication has pros and cons, depending on the patient's situation. Your doctor will use information about you and your seizures to choose a medication that will likely work for your specific case. Some types of seizures respond better to certain medications than to others. Despite the abundance of information about each available antiseizure medication, your doctor can't accurately predict whether a medication will work for you. Some people respond better to certain medications than to others.

SIDE EFFECTS

Each type of medication has potential side effects, but that doesn't mean they happen in every person who takes them. Some side effects may be barely noticeable, while others may be intolerable or even dangerous. Your doctor will take possible side effects into consideration before choosing a medication for you. While you are taking the medication, your doctor will check in with you regularly and may conduct blood or urine tests to make sure your body is handling the medication well.

Some medications cause sleepiness, hyperactivity, and other problems that interfere with schoolwork and other activities. Antiseizure medications can also affect a person's mood. Some medications can adversely affect internal organs. If you are having any unusual symptoms, talk to your doctor. Many of these problems can be corrected with a change in

CHOOSING NOT TO MEDICATE

People with very infrequent or mild seizures may choose not to take medication to treat their epilepsy. Even if your seizures hardly affect your daily life, it is important to work with your doctor to determine if and how you will proceed with treatment.

dosage or medication, but it's best to catch the problem early.

If you have a rash, call your doctor's office immediately. A rash can indicate an allergic response to the medication, which can develop into a dangerous reaction. An allergic reaction can happen even if you've been taking the medication for many months.

If taken during pregnancy, some antiseizure medications can pose risks to the developing baby. Before becoming pregnant, or as soon as a woman realizes she is pregnant, it is important to consult with a doctor to decide what course of action is safest for both the pregnant woman and the developing baby. To prevent or minimize the risk to a developing baby, it is advised that women with epilepsy plan pregnancies, discuss options with their doctor, and take action to prevent problems before becoming pregnant.

BIRTH CONTROL AND ANTISEIZURE MEDS

Women take birth control pills for many reasons besides preventing pregnancy. Birth control pills can help moderate bad cramps or make an unpredictable cycle more regular. If you are taking birth control pills, it is important that your neurologist knows you are taking them. Birth control and antiseizure medications can interact in a variety of ways, and in some cases either one can be made less effective. Other medications can also interact with your antiseizure meds, so it's important to tell your neurologist about all medications you are taking.

FORGETTING TO TAKE YOUR MEDICINE

Although medication can help control your seizures, it doesn't cure epilepsy. If you stop taking your medication or miss a dose, seizures can return. Develop a routine or method to make sure you remember to take your medication. Tape a note to the mirror in the bathroom, set an alarm on your cell phone or watch, put your meds right next to your glasses—figure out what works for you. But even if you have a great system down, it's still possible you will forget to take a dose one day. Check with your doctor to make sure you know what to do if you forget to take your medication.

IF MEDICATION DOESN'T WORK

Approximately 20 to 30 percent of people with epilepsy have seizures that are considered intractable.[3] This means they cannot be controlled with one or more medications. People with intractable epilepsy should

DOSAGE CHANGES

As you grow and your body changes size and shape, your doctor may need to change the dosage of your medication. If your seizures start to return, your doctor might raise your dosage. On the other hand, if seizures remain under control despite a decreased relative amount of medicine in your blood, your doctor might keep your dosage the same. Over time, your doctor may be able to help you decrease your dosage or even stop the medication.

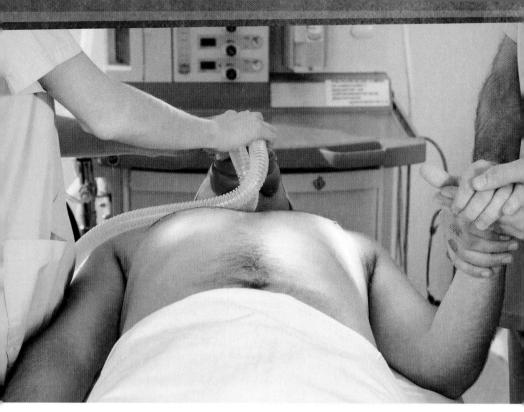

For epilepsy that can't be controlled with medication, surgery may be an option to treat seizures.

work with a neurologist and, if possible, see an epileptologist for specialized treatment.

SURGERY

For some people with intractable epilepsy, surgery may be an option. Whether surgery can be considered depends on the specifics of a person's epilepsy. Surgery may be a promising option when there is a known and isolated location within the brain where a person's seizure activity begins. Surgery is conducted such that it will not affect other parts of the brain or compromise other brain functions. Brain surgery is scary, but the risks associated with the surgery are low. For people with severe uncontrolled seizures, the risks of brain surgery can be less than the risks associated with ongoing uncontrolled seizures.

VAGUS NERVE STIMULATION

Vagus nerve stimulation (VNS) is a treatment used to prevent seizures by sending electric impulses to the brain via the vagus nerve. The VNS device is implanted in the chest and connected by a wire to the vagus nerve in the neck. VNS was first used in 1988 to treat epilepsy in patients who didn't respond to other treatments. In the following decade, several clinical studies demonstrated that VNS was safe and that it reduced seizure frequency in some people. In 1997, VNS became an approved epilepsy treatment in the United States. More recent studies show that VNS can have benefits in addition to the reduction of seizure frequency. VNS can also reduce the length of a typical seizure and shorten the recovery time a person needs after the seizure is over.

KETOGENIC DIET

Your body uses the food you eat as fuel. If the body is starved of carbohydrates, it enters a state called ketosis. When ketosis sets in, the body starts breaking down fat for fuel. Ketosis often causes seizures to stop, though no one knows exactly why. The ketogenic diet is a treatment typically only considered for people whose seizures are difficult to control with medication.

The ketogenic diet is not something you can simply try at home! It requires the oversight of a team of specialists, including a doctor, a dietician, a nurse, and others. Forcing your body to enter ketosis isn't easy. People using ketosis as a treatment must adhere to a very strict, very precise, very high fat diet. The ketogenic diet can also cause several complications, including kidney stones, constipation, vitamin deficiencies, and slowed growth. For some patients, a doctor may suggest the modified Atkins diet or the low glycemic index diet. These are slightly less

CHARLIE ABRAHAMS

Charlie Abrahams had intractable epilepsy as a baby, but he also had the good fortune of working with medical staff at Johns Hopkins Hospital in the early 1990s to try a ketogenic diet. Charlie started the diet when he was almost three years old, and it worked. His family started the Charlie Foundation, an organization dedicated to increasing awareness of the ketogenic diet. After successfully controlling Charlie's epilepsy, Charlie's family wanted to extend hope and provide information to other families struggling with intractable epilepsy. Visit www.charliefoundation.org or look for "Charlie's Speech" on YouTube to hear the story for yourself.

restrictive diets that may also reduce seizure frequency. Like the ketogenic diet, however, these treatments require the supervision of a team of health-care professionals.

ADDITIONAL THINGS YOU CAN DO

In addition to pursuing medical treatment, it is important for people with epilepsy to maintain a healthy and active lifestyle. Eat a nutritious diet, but don't go overboard on vitamin and mineral supplements. A variety of fruits, vegetables, whole grains, lean meats, and dairy products should give you the balanced nutrients you need. Try eating fish once in a while, or add flax seeds to your diet. These foods contain omega-3 fatty acids, which may improve brain function. Make sure to eat regularly, because skipping meals can increase your risk of having a seizure. Caffeine and artificial sweeteners can also trigger seizures, so limit your intake. It is especially important for people with epilepsy not to use alcohol, tobacco, or other drugs that can trigger seizures or interfere with medication.

Evidence suggests that physical activity can reduce the frequency of a person's seizures, though it's not entirely clear why. It's possible that exercise makes the brain more active, and an active brain is less susceptible to seizures. It's also possible that the chemicals your body releases during exercise, such as endorphins,

Some activities can be significantly more dangerous for a person with epilepsy.

somehow prevent seizures. Plus, exercise has all sorts of additional health benefits. There's scientific evidence that exercise can improve mood, reduce anxiety, and overall improve a person's outlook on life! That said, depending on how well your seizures are controlled, certain activities might not be worth the risk. Extreme sports, water sports, and activities likely to cause head injuries are especially dangerous.

And don't forget to do your best to avoid risk factors. Managing stress levels and getting enough sleep can greatly reduce the risk of seizures.

ASK YOURSELF THIS

- *What have your experiences with medication been like? If you are on medication now, have you experienced any side effects?*

- *Have you, or has anyone you know, been on the ketogenic diet? What was it like for you, or what do you know about the other person's experience?*

- *Of the additional things you can do to help control your seizures, which do you already do? Which could you improve on? Explain.*

- *If you have intractable epilepsy, would you consider surgery to control your seizures? Why or why not?*

- *Have you experienced unusual mood swings or symptoms of anxiety or depression as a result of your epilepsy or medication? If so, how did you cope with these issues? If not, has your epilepsy or medication brought on other health challenges?*

YOUR LIFE: MANAGING EPILEPSY

During high school, Stacey worried about what other people would think if she had a seizure. She also worried about when the next seizure would happen. She knew she couldn't control what was going on in her body, but there was always this feeling of anxiety

Epilepsy does not have to limit your life.

about the next seizure. Where would it occur? Who would be there? What would happen? As best she could, Stacey pushed these thoughts out of her mind. She was sure it would be easier to move forward in her life if she didn't dwell on the possibility of a seizure.

Stacey joined different school activities: drama, choir, flag corps, German club, and a few others. She made some great friends. Outside school, Stacey studied karate and worked part-time as an instructor. Stacey made a few small changes in her life. She talked to friends about her epilepsy. She liked to sit near the aisle in her classrooms, and she preferred to be by the door. It just made her feel safer. She figured if she had a seizure during class, there were fewer things she might hit if she sat at the end of a row. And if there were ever a medical emergency, being by the door would allow help to get to her easily. Over time, epilepsy settled into a comfortable place in Stacey's life. Sure, it's a part of Stacey's life. But it's certainly not the defining factor.

TAKING CONTROL

Living well with epilepsy isn't just about seizure control. Epilepsy can affect your school life, your social life, your family life, and your work life. It can affect the sports and activities you participate in and the way you get from one place to another. In short, in can affect your whole life. Living well with epilepsy means identifying and addressing concerns you have and making healthy choices. Most important, living well with epilepsy means living your life. Don't forget that even if there are certain things you can't do (such as getting your driver's license right now, maybe), there are infinitely more things you can do.

TALK WITH YOUR DOCTORS

If you are suffering from depression or anxiety, or if you have any other psychological concerns, it is extremely important to talk to a medical professional. It's one thing to have a bad day

CHANDA GUNN

Chanda Gunn refuses to let anything get in her way, especially her epilepsy. She began having seizures when she was in fourth grade but was able to control them with medication. In college, her seizures came back. She loved playing ice hockey, but her coach didn't want her on the team. Gunn's doctor changed her medication and upped her dosage to get her seizures back under control. Today, Chanda Gunn is a goalie for the USA Women's Hockey Team and a spokesperson for the Epilepsy Therapy Project. She even won a bronze medal in the 2006 Winter Olympics. "I've learned to live with it," she says, "the fear of the unknown, because I want to really *live* life and for me living means playing ice hockey."[1]

now and then, or to worry about a big test or event. But if these feelings stick around and interfere with your daily life, it's a big deal. Your doctor can help you develop a plan to address the situation. Depression and anxiety are not your fault, and they're not illnesses you can just get over. They are illnesses that can block your perception of reality. Thankfully, these illnesses can improve with treatment. Certain antiseizure drugs can affect your mood. When this happens, a change in medication may improve the situation.

Talk with your doctors about any other concerns you have, too. If you have questions about medications, side effects, safety, risks—anything at all—bring them up at your next appointment. There may be things you'd rather talk to your doctor about alone. That's okay.

IMPROVING EPILEPSY MANAGEMENT

With the goal of improving epilepsy care and treatment, the American Academy of Neurology (AAN) developed a set of eight performance measures, published in 2011. Directed at doctors, the performance measures are intended to provide guidelines for consistency and thoroughness in treatment. The measures include thorough documentation of patient symptoms, use of an EEG and MRI or CT scan, discussion of medication side effects, safety issues, and women's issues. Ask your doctor if she or he is familiar with the AAN practice guidelines.

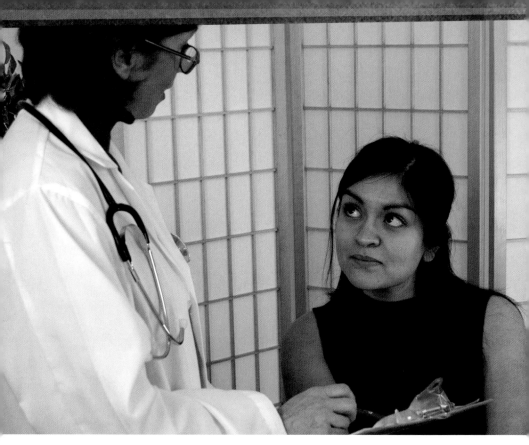

It is important to be open with your doctor about any concerns you may have about your epilepsy.

If a family member comes with you to see the doctor, let that person know you'd like to have a private discussion with your doctor. You might have a million questions but forget them each time you have a doctor's appointment. If so, keep a list and take it with you so you don't miss anything.

KEEP A LOG

Keeping a record or log of your seizures can be a helpful way for you and your doctors to understand your particular brand of epilepsy. You can get a journal and divide it into sections. In one section, you can keep track of your seizures: the dates they occur, what time of day they occur, their duration, what you were doing when they started, and any other relevant details. In another section, you can keep track of information related to your medication. Make a note if you ever forget to take a dose. Keep notes on any side effects or changes you are experiencing. This log will help you keep accurate and detailed information about your epilepsy, which will help your doctor provide you with the best possible treatment.

Being informed about epilepsy and your body allows you to take control of your life and make the best decisions about managing your epilepsy. Look online at the Epilepsy Foundation Web site. Check out the other references at the end of this book. Ask your doctor for more references and about local epilepsy groups. Ask

COMMON MISCONCEPTIONS

Epilepsy is a mental illness. Whereas psychologists or psychiatrists treat mental illnesses, neurologists treat epilepsy.

Epilepsy affects your intelligence. Aristotle even believed epilepsy was connected with genius.[2]

Epilepsy is contagious. In case there was any question, you can't catch epilepsy from or spread it to others.

Some seizure response dogs can sense an oncoming seizure, giving their owners time to prepare.

a librarian to help you find information about epilepsy. Talk to your family and to your doctor to learn more about your specific diagnosis, test results, and treatments.

ASK YOURSELF THIS

- *Do you keep a log of your seizures and your experiences with medication? How* has it helped you, or how do you think it would help you?

- What part of your condition do you want to learn more about? What will you do to find out what you want to know?

- Has anyone ever called 911 while you were having a seizure? If so, why?

- What do you feel is the most difficult aspect of epilepsy to manage? What is the easiest?

- Have you let your friends know what to do when you have a seizure? If so, how did they respond to the information? Do you feel safer now that they know? If you haven't told them, why not? How could you bring up the topic?

SEIZURE RESPONSE DOGS

Seizure response dogs are professionally trained as companions for people with epilepsy. The main service a seizure response dog provides is to alert others when a person is having a seizure. The dog may bark or run to alert other people. Some say their dog lets them know when they are about to have a seizure. They believe their dogs can recognize a chemical or behavioral signal that precedes the seizure. A seizure response dog can provide the comfort and confidence some people with epilepsy need to feel safe. Having a dog is a major responsibility, but it can greatly improve the lives of some people with epilepsy.

WHAT WILL HAPPEN NEXT?

A mala volunteers at a nearby nursing home. One of her favorite residents is Marie, a 96-year-old woman. Amala and Marie spend lots of time talking, and one day Amala told Marie she had epilepsy. It turned out that Marie's best friend from childhood had

Epilepsy research continues to improve treatment.
Young people with epilepsy have a promising future.

epilepsy, too. Marie's experience with epilepsy was a world apart from Amala's experience. Marie loves hearing all about Amala's tests and treatments. She quizzes her about her visits to the doctor. It sounds like epilepsy was a much larger obstacle for Marie's friend than it is for Amala.

When Marie was young, epilepsy was less understood, and very few antiseizure medications were available. Marie's friend didn't attend school because of her "condition." Amala, on the other hand, was elected to serve in her school's student council. She is a member of the improv comedy club and the yoga club. She has a 3.8 grade point average and hopes to raise that before she applies to college. Her discussions with Marie make her curious about what it will be like to have epilepsy in another 20, 50, or even 70 years. What will treatments be like then? Will there be a cure? Will public

EPILEPSY AWARENESS

The Epilepsy Foundation conducted the first campaign for epilepsy awareness in 1968. In 2003, the US Congress unanimously passed a resolution declaring November as National Epilepsy Awareness Month. Epilepsy Awareness Month includes fund-raisers and educational programs for the public, families, schools, and professionals.

perception of epilepsy change? Will research provide more insight into how and why seizures occur and epilepsy develops? She guesses she will have to wait and see.

EPILEPSY TODAY

Looking back at what we've learned in the last several decades of epilepsy research, the view is pretty amazing. We've started to make sense of some cases of epilepsy through detailed studies of genetics. We've transformed our ability to produce images of the brain. We've mastered certain types of brain surgery. We've done all this and more. As exciting as it is to think about how far we've come, it's even more exciting to think about where we are going. What will we learn in the upcoming years and decades? As we learn more about epilepsy and seizures, treatments can be improved. We might even take radically new approaches to treatment.

EPILEPSY RESEARCH GOALS

Several conferences have brought members of the epilepsy community—including doctors, nurses, researchers, people with epilepsy, and their families—together to discuss the needs of the community and how best to address them. Attendees came up with goals for the epilepsy research community to pursue in the years ahead. Resources are specifically devoted to monitoring and continuing to work toward the following goals:

1. Prevent epilepsy and its progression.

2. Develop new therapeutic strategies and optimize current approaches to cure epilepsy.

3. Prevent, limit, and reverse accompanying disorders such as depression, anxiety, and learning challenges associated with epilepsy and its treatment.[1]

PREVENTING EPILEPSY

We know that people who have head injuries or other risk factors have a greater chance of developing epilepsy. There is often an interval of several months to years between the head injury or other event that leaves the brain susceptible to seizures and the actual onset of epilepsy. Some

PREVENTING SUDEP

Epilepsy itself is not deadly, but sudden unexplained death in epilepsy (SUDEP) is a cause of death for approximately 1 out of 1,000 people with epilepsy. As the name suggests, SUDEP is hard to anticipate, hard to study, and therefore essentially impossible to prevent. As epilepsy research continues, perhaps an improved understanding of how and why seizures occur can aid in the study of SUDEP. If research can help to identify why SUDEP occurs, there's hope that it could be stopped.

researchers are hoping to learn more about what happens in this interim time period. The technical term for the development of epilepsy, which occurs in this interim, is epileptogenesis. One of the primary goals of researchers today is to figure out whether it is possible to prevent epilepsy from developing, and if so, how. Perhaps medications, electric stimulation, physical therapies, or other interventions could interrupt epileptogenesis, and therefore prevent epilepsy. Learning more about the causes of epilepsy could also lead to prevention methods.

PARTICIPATING IN STUDIES

Has your doctor ever asked if you wanted to participate in a study? Researchers gather information about epilepsy, including the effectiveness of medications, by using data from volunteer participants. Some studies carry risks, so discuss the topic thoroughly with your doctor and your family. If you are comfortable with the study and decide to join in, your participation may contribute to the next breakthrough in epilepsy research!

NEW AND IMPROVED TREATMENTS

New antiseizure medications will likely be coming on the market in the years and decades ahead. Improved medications will be more effective or have fewer side effects. They may also have different effects on the body and brain than existing antiseizure

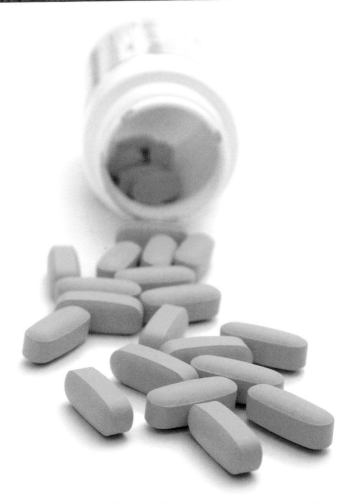

New medications and treatments will help manage epilepsy better than ever before.

medicines. New medications could help control seizures for people who do not respond to existing forms of treatment.

Brain stimulation is a new treatment currently under research. An implanted device sends electric stimulation directly into the brain. The results look promising, but researchers still have many questions. Studies could help determine which parts of the brain are most responsive to stimulation. Other new treatments may involve new surgery techniques, stem cell transplants, influencing the growth of neurons, and gene replacement.

WILL THERE EVER BE A CURE?

Well, maybe. In part, it depends on what is meant by "cure." Some people say epilepsy is cured when a patient has "no seizures, no side effects." Technically the person still has epilepsy, but it is effectively cured. However, when people say something is "cured," they usually mean it is gone. Still, no seizures and no side effects sounds like a cure most people could live with. The development of a permanent cure will require a much more thorough understanding of how epilepsy develops, and how and why seizures occur.

ADDRESSING COMORBIDITIES

A comorbidity is a condition or illness that occurs alongside another condition or illness. For people with epilepsy, there's an increased chance of having certain other conditions, including depression and migraines. Many epilepsy comorbidities are psychological conditions, but they may also be medical conditions. Comorbidities can compound the struggles that epilepsy presents. Improved understanding of how and why comorbidities occur could lead to an ability to treat or cure them, and perhaps even to prevent their development.

ASK YOURSELF THIS

- *Which direction in epilepsy research is most important to you? Why?*

- *Would you be interested in being a researcher who studies epilepsy? Why or why not?*

- *Do you think the three research goals described in this chapter effectively summarize research needs for epilepsy? Why or why not? What would you add?*

- *Would you be interested in participating in a research study about epilepsy? Why or why not?*

- *November is National Epilepsy Awareness Month. Next November, what will you do to help increase awareness of epilepsy?*

FRIENDS AND FAMILY: DEALING WITH SOCIAL ISSUES

Kevin and Shayla had been dating for almost two months. At school, they often ate lunch together. After school, they both had practice, so they sometimes met up afterward. Shayla would be turning 16 in just a few months. Kevin was already 16, so

Don't be afraid to tell someone you trust about your epilepsy.

she kept asking him about his license. So far, Kevin had avoided answering. He would give a flirtatious smile and say something silly, or put on a serious face and say, "I told you, the cops won't let me." He joked on the outside, but on the inside, he hated when the topic came up. He knew he'd have to talk about it eventually. Or maybe he would just break up with her. He really liked Shayla, but sometimes he felt like he should just end things so they wouldn't have to have the dreaded epilepsy conversation.

One Friday, he and Shayla missed the bus and were sitting around waiting for their parents to pick them up. Kevin decided to tell her. Once, he had told another girl he was dating and it didn't go very well. Nothing really happened, but the conversation was sort of awkward and they didn't really talk much afterward. This time it was totally different. Shayla laughed, but in a good way. "I knew there was something about that driver's license!" she said. "Why didn't you tell me?" And it was so crazy. It turned out Shayla has a cousin with epilepsy, and her cousin has the same kind of seizures Kevin does. After that, things were totally normal between them. Well, actually, it was way better than normal. Now that Shayla knew, Kevin was free of that dread

Most teenagers—not just teens with epilepsy— have disagreements with siblings and parents.

he'd been carrying around. He was able to be himself, totally and completely.

TALKING WITH YOUR FAMILY

When it comes to family stuff, you probably want to have a little more freedom and don't want your parents, guardians, or other family members breathing down your neck. Other teenagers have disagreements with parents. But for adolescents with epilepsy, there's an additional set of potential arguments to take up with parents.

Your family might be a little overprotective of you. They might not realize that you are totally capable of doing most things. But here's the thing: parents and other family members are watching you transform from a child to a young adult. They know all about you as a child, but they are just getting to know you as a young adult. For starters, try showing your family that you are responsible. Take your medication on time, every day. Keep up with expectations at home and at school. Be proactive about managing your epilepsy. These actions will prove that you can handle more responsibility.

If you aren't currently in charge of your own treatment, start on a path to take on more responsibility. You could make a deal with your parents: you will keep track of when to take your medication, but you will report to your parent that you did so. This way, you can eliminate the nagging parent part of things and demonstrate that you are, in fact, able to do this for yourself. And you'll have a backup. In case you forget to take your medicine and don't check in, your parent will know to contact you with a reminder.

When you are feeling frustrated with your family, take a deep breath. Realize that they aren't trying to make your life difficult. They care about you and want to make sure you are safe. Your family is an important part of your support network. It might not always feel like it, but they really are on your team. They want to help you achieve your goals.

In some cases, it can be a big help to bring a third party into the conversation. This third party could be your doctor, but if not, it should be someone who understands epilepsy and is familiar with your particular condition. This person can reassure your parents and help them understand that, with a few compromises involved, you should be allowed to live your own life.

TALKING WITH FRIENDS AND PEERS

It's your choice who to tell about your epilepsy. How much you choose to talk about it can depend on many things: when your seizures usually happen, how frequently your seizures happen, how long you've known a person, and other considerations. Some of your friends may know all sorts of things about you—your favorite foods, your shoe size, and what song is always stuck in your head, to name a few. These are the friends you've probably already told about your epilepsy. If you haven't, well, why haven't you? Think about telling them. It can be a relief to have it out in the open. If you ever have a seizure when your friends are around, it won't be a surprise to them. They will be able to help you through a seizure and let others know what's going on. Your friends are your advocates and your support network for many things in your life—including epilepsy.

Being able to talk comfortably about your epilepsy is important. It helps if you are well informed about epilepsy in general and your particular circumstance. This allows you to answer questions with confidence and help dispel misconceptions other people might have. If you can talk openly and honestly with your friends, they might feel like they can open up to you, too.

Some people you know might be inconsiderate about your epilepsy. They probably aren't people who make good friends anyway. Just remember that's their problem, not yours. People who

LOSING BLADDER CONTROL

Some people lose bladder control during a seizure. In fact, it might be one of the most dreaded parts of having a seizure in public. If it will make you feel more confident, you can urinate more frequently so you won't have a full bladder if you do have a seizure. But please, don't let your bladder take over your life! Nobody really cares. Honestly, people who aren't used to seeing seizures are going to be a little freaked out when they see you have a seizure. They are going to be relieved to see you are okay.

are mean or hateful very likely have emotional problems and deep insecurities that cause them to act inappropriately. If classmates ever bother you in ways that make you feel unsafe or uncomfortable at school, talk to a teacher, principal, or other trusted adult at your school. It is your right to feel safe and comfortable at school.

USING COMMON SENSE

Are you debating whether it is safe for a person with epilepsy to ride a bicycle? It doesn't really make sense to ask whether "a person with epilepsy" can safely ride a bicycle. One person with epilepsy might have 150 absence seizures each day. Or another person might have had no seizures for the last 14 months. Clearly, the safety of an activity depends on

WILL I EVER BE ABLE TO DRIVE?

The laws about driving with epilepsy are different for each state. You can contact the Department of Motor Vehicles in your state to find out what laws apply to you. In most cases, you can get a license and drive as long as you have not had any seizures for a particular amount of time, typically six months. Your doctor will also probably be familiar with the laws. Having a seizure behind the wheel could be very dangerous for you, your passengers, pedestrians, and other drivers. If you are driving, always take your medication on schedule so your seizures stay controlled. Cars are dangerous—even if there's no epilepsy involved! More teens die from car accidents than from any other cause.[1]

each individual's circumstance.

Instead, you might discuss with your parents whether it's safe for *you* to ride your bicycle. That's where you need to use common sense. Everything carries risks. Depending on your particular circumstance, riding a bike may be as risky for you as it is for any other adolescent. If your seizures aren't entirely under control, it might be reasonable to ride your bike for short distances on the bike path. But it might not be reasonable to do long-distance road racing. Do you always have an aura before seizures? If so, you could get off your bike and sit down if you felt a seizure coming on. Did you just switch medication? If so, you probably have no idea yet whether it is effective in preventing seizures. Make your safety decisions on an individual basis.

It can be helpful to bring in an informed third party to help resolve conflicts with parents. A third party can help everyone remember to

TACKLING EPILEPSY

Before his retirement in 2011, Alan Faneca played for the Pittsburgh Steelers, the New York Jets, and the Arizona Cardinals. Jason Snelling is a running back for the Atlanta Falcons. What do these two men have in common, besides their professional football careers? You guessed it: epilepsy. They were both diagnosed as teenagers. More recently, they have both worked with the Epilepsy Foundation to help educate and inspire others.

use common sense. It's really important to stay safe. This means you might have to make some compromises. But it's critical that your parents let you (and that you let yourself) live your life.

ASK YOURSELF THIS

- *What is the biggest social issue caused by epilepsy that you struggle with? If you don't have epilepsy, what do you think the biggest social issue would be if you did?*

- *Think about a time when you told a friend about your epilepsy, or a friend told you about her or his epilepsy. What was the conversation like? How did it change your relationship with that person?*

- *Have you ever lost bladder control during a seizure? How did you react? Did people notice? If it hasn't happened to you, do you think about it? How do you think you would feel if it happened?*

- *What do you wish you could do that your parents*

WILL I EVER BE ABLE TO HAVE CHILDREN?

Yes, people with epilepsy can and do have children. Epilepsy is not known to affect a man's role in conception. For women with epilepsy, pregnancy can present some complications. Antiseizure medications can cause birth defects, so it is especially important for women to plan their pregnancies to minimize risks.

Telling trusted and supportive friends about your epilepsy can be a relief.

won't allow you to do or that you don't feel comfortable doing because of your epilepsy? What steps can you take toward making this thing possible?

• Has anyone ever teased or bullied you because of your epilepsy? If so, how did you react? How would you react if someone teased you now? If not, how do you think you would react if this happened?

HELP! HELPING YOURSELF AND OTHERS

G arin now has a total of 20 people on his team—eight family members, himself included, and 12 friends. They are renting two big vans to drive to Washington, DC, for the National Walk for Epilepsy, and everyone is giddy with excitement. Marissa and Ellie

*The support of family and friends can make
managing your epilepsy much easier.*

have already claimed the back seat of one van. Matt is bringing a game he wants everyone to play during the drive out there, but he won't tell anyone what it is. He says they'll find out once the trip starts. Garin brought his unicycle for the parade. He's been practicing and can stay on for pretty much as long as he wants to now—he doesn't lose his balance anymore. He thought it would be fun to bring. Maybe he'll get a few laughs. Garin is also excited to see some friends he met at camp who are doing the walk, too. These friends were the first people he met who also had epilepsy. They had an awesome summer at camp together, and this trip is going to be amazing, too.

Garin remembers what it was like right after he was diagnosed with epilepsy. He was really scared. At that point, he didn't know much about epilepsy. In retrospect, he realizes that the unknown was a major part of what made everything so scary! It's easy to get freaked out when you have no idea what's going on. He remembers a few people who were really helpful right after the diagnosis. Of course, friends and family were cool, but they were in the same clueless boat as he was. Some of the people who helped Garin most were strangers he saw in videos or met online. Garin found tons of videos of teenagers talking about epilepsy on the Epilepsy Foundation Web site and on www.epilepsy.com. The videos answered many of Garin's questions. And when he posted on forums about his diagnosis, a bunch of people responded. They knew exactly what he was going through, and they were really supportive. Now that Garin is well beyond his diagnosis, with his seizures under control, he has started volunteering with a local organization that provides epilepsy education in schools and for the public. It's been so great to actually meet other people who have epilepsy. He wishes he had met these people earlier! With his experience, Garin feels like he could offer support to other kids with epilepsy—especially kids who were recently diagnosed and are still trying to figure it all out. He loves helping people who are newly diagnosed connect with other people with epilepsy. Garin remembers vividly how important that was for him.

HELPING YOURSELF

Your epilepsy questions have been answered. You have worked out a seizure management plan with your doctor. You're taking good care of yourself and, if you have medication, you're taking it regularly. You are off to a great start, but you can go so much further! There are ways for you to work through challenges, find ways around obstacles, and live life to the fullest. You might also consider helping others. Helping others is a great way to help yourself, too.

A MEDICAL ID TAG

Whether your seizures are rare or frequent, it's human nature to worry. You might worry, and your parents and other family members might worry. Some people feel more confident, free, or secure when they wear a medical ID tag. This is usually worn on a bracelet or necklace and contains information about your medical conditions. It might, for example, say that a person has epilepsy (or another condition), identify the medication the person uses, and provide a telephone number of a family member or doctor. Medical staff (and some nonmedical folks) know to check for a medical ID tag. If a person is alone and has a seizure (or other medical event),

REALITY CHECK

Approximately one in five young people lives in poverty.[1] Almost one in four teenagers has migraines.[2] And one in four young people has a food allergy.[3] Almost one out of 50 young people is a victim of physical abuse or maltreatment.[4] Many teens live with diabetes, learning disabilities, cancer, and other health challenges, including epilepsy. All around you, young people like you are facing challenges, asking for help, being brave, and learning to cope.

the tag can provide the necessary information to eliminate the guesswork and let medical staff know what's going on.

Not everyone likes medical ID tags, however. Some people feel they are an unwelcome advertisement of a medical condition. And some just don't like wearing a bracelet or necklace all the time. But many others get peace of mind wearing a medical ID bracelet. It also helps parents feel more secure in allowing their teens greater freedom.

SET THE BAR HIGH AND KNOW YOUR RIGHTS

With a few exceptions (being an airline pilot or bus driver, for example), having epilepsy does not exclude you from being a candidate for a job. People with epilepsy have careers doing nearly everything and anything you can imagine. You can, too.

When you apply or interview for a job, you do not need to provide information about your epilepsy. If you are offered the job, you can choose whether to tell your employer and coworkers about your condition. You have the right to request reasonable accommodations if needed.

Discrimination because of epilepsy is illegal, but unfortunately, it sometimes happens. If

Participating in the National Walk for Epilepsy is a great way to raise awareness and meet other teens with epilepsy.

you are a victim of discrimination because of epilepsy, you may find support and assistance from the Epilepsy Legal Defense Fund.

CONNECT WITH OTHERS

Especially right after the initial diagnosis, (but certainly at other times, too!) it's possible to feel kind of alone. One way to connect with others who have epilepsy is through local epilepsy organizations. Check out the Epilepsy Foundation Web site to find out if there's an organization near you. Local chapters may host retreats, camps, school programs, informal gatherings, conferences, and other events. There may be support groups, and possibly even a group for teens! See what's offered in your area.

Whether or not there's a local organization in your area, you can easily connect with other people with epilepsy online as long as you have access to the Internet. If you don't have Internet access at home, there is probably free Internet at your local public or school library. If not, ask a teacher if there's a computer with Internet that you can use after school. This can be a great way to talk with others about experiences with epilepsy. But remember, forums are places for people to give opinions, not where you should get your medical advice! Many people find strength and support, friendship and fun, by connecting with other people (either in person or online) who have had similar experiences. (Always remember to be safe

ART THERAPY

Art therapy can help you express the thoughts and feelings you have about your epilepsy. This creative outlet helps you work through problems and boost your self-esteem. It can help reduce stress, which may reduce the frequency of your seizures. Art therapy focus groups can also be great places to form friendships with other teens with epilepsy.

online and not give out personally identifying information!)

FIND A SUMMER CAMP

Have you ever been to summer camp? It can be awesome! For teens with epilepsy, it can be important to attend a camp with professionals prepared to help manage seizures. Although some camps don't have the staff or training to assist with seizure management, many camps do. And some camps are designed specifically to serve youth with epilepsy. Search the Epilepsy Foundation's Web site to find a camp near you. Camp can be a great opportunity to meet other teens from near and far, some of whom have epilepsy. Camps offer loads of different activities, from rock climbing to knitting and everything in between. Scholarships may be available if you don't have the cash to go.

REACH OUT TO OTHERS

Have you ever met someone who really made a difference in your life? If you feel ready to reach out to others who have epilepsy, *you* can be the one who makes a difference. You've overcome obstacles as you've learned to live well with epilepsy. You've found ways to manage ongoing challenges. Your experience with epilepsy can be an inspiration to others.

If your town already has a social or support group for teens with epilepsy, consider getting involved. You could mentor younger members or start an annual fund-raiser or social event. If your town doesn't have a group for teens, well, maybe it's time for you to start one! Of course, you wouldn't have to do it alone. Talk with family members, teachers and other staff at your school, your friends, and anyone else who might lend a hand.

LOOKING AHEAD

What might the future hold for your life with epilepsy? Unfortunately, that's not certain. Some people may struggle to manage their seizures for the rest of their lives. Others will never have a seizure again. Still others will find they can manage their seizures with medicine and healthy lifestyle choices. And who knows, there

DJ HAPA

DJ Hapa is a celebrity DJ from Los Angeles. Hapa attended UCLA after being awarded a scholarship. He gave the keynote speech at his own graduation. In addition to traveling the world for high-profile events, Hapa is a director and instructor for a DJ academy he founded. Oh, and he also has epilepsy, which was diagnosed in high school. At age 26, Hapa became the spokesperson for the Epilepsy Therapy Project. Hapa is passionate about increasing awareness about epilepsy and about spreading the message that "you can have epilepsy and you can succeed."[5]

may even be a cure around the corner! The future is yours to shape. Armed with information and skills about living well with epilepsy, you are ready for anything. It's your life and you're in charge. Enjoy life, be safe, and have fun!

ASK YOURSELF THIS

- *What ways have you found to help yourself that aren't mentioned in this book?*

- *How has living with epilepsy allowed you to connect with or help others? How do you plan to help others with epilepsy in the future?*

- *If you wear a medical ID tag, how do you feel about it? If not, what do you do to help keep yourself or others from worrying?*

- *What do you plan to do to help inform your friends or others about either your epilepsy specifically or epilepsy in general?*

- *What do you want your life to look like in five years? What about ten years? What will you do to get there?*

JUST THE FACTS

Seizures define epilepsy and can take many forms. Seizures may or may not involve a loss of consciousness.

In most cases, there is no apparent cause of a person's epilepsy. In some cases, the cause can be identified and may include severe head injury, brain infection, stroke, tumors, or structural abnormalities of the brain.

A diagnosis of epilepsy depends heavily on personal accounts describing seizures. Epilepsy is typically diagnosed after two or more seizures. Information from blood tests, EEGs, CT scans, or MRIs may be used to confirm the diagnosis.

An EEG measures the patterns of electric activity in a person's brain. MRIs and CT scans show details of brain structure.

Seizures may be partial, in which case the seizure activity is restricted to a particular part of the brain, or generalized, in which case the seizure activity spreads throughout the brain. Seizures may begin as partial seizures but progress to generalized seizures.

Approximately 70 percent of people with epilepsy successfully control seizures with medication. Surgery may be an option for some. For intractable cases, vagus nerve stimulation, a ketogenic diet, and other approaches may decrease seizure frequency.

Seizures occur when there is an irregular electric discharge in your brain.

In most cases, seizures do not have permanent effects on the brain. Extended or prolonged seizures, however, may cause permanent damage.

Stress, sleep deprivation, nutritional deficiencies, illness, use of drugs or alcohol, and irregularities in antiseizure medication use can all increase a person's chances of having a seizure.

Regular physical activity, a nutritionally balanced diet, and limited caffeine intake can help minimize a person's chances of having a seizure.

Decisions about personal safety must be made on an individual basis. They should take into account the type of seizures a person has and whether the seizures are controlled. Certain activities, such as driving, are subject to state laws.

The daily impact of epilepsy depends on the individual, the type of epilepsy, and whether seizures are under control. Epilepsy may have essentially no impact on some people's daily lives, while seizures may constantly interrupt the lives of others.

It is not possible for a person to swallow her or his tongue. It is, however, dangerous to put something in the mouth of a person having a seizure.

Epilepsy is not a mental illness.

Between 0.5 percent and 2 percent of people will be diagnosed with epilepsy at some point in their lives.

WHERE TO TURN

If You Are There When Someone Has a Seizure

When someone has a seizure, remember to keep calm. Check for a medical ID bracelet. Time the duration of the seizure. On the rare occasion a seizure lasts longer than five minutes, you need to call 911 for emergency help. Reassure others by letting them know it is just a seizure and the person will be fine. Clear the area around the person of objects that could cause injury, and loosen any neckwear. Use a jacket or blanket to cushion the person's head, and carefully roll the person onto her or his side. After the seizure is over, the person may need some time to fully regain alertness. Sit down with the person. Be ready to talk and let the person know what happened. It is helpful to stay with the person until she or he feels fully alert again.

If You Are Trying to Gain Control of Your Seizures

You can provide your doctor with critical information by keeping detailed records of your seizures and when they occur, when you take or miss medication, and any side effects you experience. If you have regular access to a computer and the Internet, you can use a free tool developed by the Epilepsy Therapy Project, called My Epilepsy Diary, to keep track of this information. What you enter in the online diary can even be sent directly to your doctor.

If You Are Trying to Achieve More Independence

There's a good chance that you have some conflicts with your parents or caregivers about what you should—or shouldn't—be allowed to do. Remember that your parents or caregivers worry because they care about you. They may be concerned that you will forget to take your medication or that you won't get enough sleep if, for example, you stay at a friend's house. Talk with your parents to negotiate the conditions that would make them comfortable and allow you to do what you hope to do. Be ready to compromise. Consider consulting with your doctor, who can give you a third-party opinion. Your doctor can give an opinion strictly about your health and well-being. The doctor may even be able to reassure your parents that the risk of having a seizure while you are camping, at the fair, or sleeping at a friend's house would probably be small.

If You Are Depressed or Contemplating Suicide

Ongoing feelings of disconnection, hopelessness, or fatigue may be symptoms of depression. People with epilepsy are at a higher risk for depression, in some cases because of medication side effects. Depression is a serious illness, but it is treatable. If you have any concerns about depression, it's very important to talk with your doctor. If your medication changes, pay attention to changes in your mood and report them to your doctor.

If you are having thoughts of suicide, don't wait to get help. Talk to an adult you trust immediately. You can also call the National Suicide Prevention Lifeline (1-800-273-8255), the USA National Suicide Hotline (1-800-SUICIDE), or the Girls & Boys Town National Hotline (1-800-448-3000) for help 24 hours a day, seven days a week.

GLOSSARY

automatism
A movement or activity that occurs during a complex partial seizure that cannot be controlled by the person having the seizure.

benign
Not harmful or dangerous.

complex partial seizure
A seizure for which electric activity is localized in a particular region of the brain, and during which a person loses consciousness.

epileptogenesis
The process by which epilepsy develops in an individual.

generalized seizure
A seizure for which electric activity is generalized throughout the brain.

neuroimaging
The use of tools, such as MRI and CT, to produce images of the brain.

neuron
A brain cell; one of the components of the nervous system.

partial seizure
A seizure for which electric activity is localized in a particular region of the brain.

simple partial seizure
A seizure for which electric activity is localized in a particular region of the brain, and during which a person maintains alertness.

vagus nerve
A nerve which begins at the brain stem and passes through the neck and chest to the stomach and abdomen.

ADDITIONAL RESOURCES

SELECTED BIBLIOGRAPHY

Bazil, Carl W. *Living Well with Epilepsy and Other Seizure Disorders.* New York: Harper Resource, 2004. Print.

Browne, Thomas R. and Gregory L. Holmes. *Handbook of Epilepsy, 3rd Edition.* Philadelphia: Lippincott Williams & Wilkins, 2004. Print.

Epilepsy Foundation. Epilepsy Foundation, n.d. Web. Jan. 2011.

epilepsy.com. epilepsy.com, n.d. Web. Jan. 2011.

Freeman, John M., Eileen P.G. Vining, and Diana J. Pillas. *Seizures and Epilepsy in Childhood: A Guide 3rd Edition.* Baltimore: Johns Hopkins Press, 2002. Print.

"NINDS Epilepsy Information Page." *National Institute of Neurological Disorders and Stroke.* National Institute of Neurological Disorders and Stroke, 6 June 2011. Web. Jan. 2011.

FURTHER READINGS

Gay, Kathlyn, and Sean McGarrahan. *Epilepsy: The Ultimate Teen Guide.* Lanham, MD: Scarecrow, 2002. Print.

Schachter, Steven C. *The Brainstorms Series, Epilepsy in Our Words: Personal Accounts of Living with Seizures.* New York: Oxford UP, 2008. Print.

Schachter, Steven C., and Lisa Francesca Andermann. *The Brainstorms Series, Epilepsy in Our World: Stories of Living with Seizures from Around the World.* New York: Oxford UP, 2008. Print.

WEB LINKS

To learn more about living with epilepsy, visit ABDO Publishing Company online at **www.abdopublishing.com**. Web sites about living with epilepsy are featured on our Book Links page. These links are routinely monitored and updated to provide the most current information available.

SOURCE NOTES

CHAPTER 1. SOMETHING'S GOING ON: SYMPTOMS AND DEFINITIONS

1. "Epilepsy and Seizure Statistics." *Epilepsy Foundation*. Epilepsy Foundation, 2010. Web. 8 Dec. 2010.

2. Ibid.

3. Steven C. Schachter. "Who Gets Epilepsy?" *epilepsy. com*. epilepsy.com, 16 Oct. 2006. Web. 8 Dec, 2010.

4. "Epilepsy and Seizure Statistics." *Epilepsy Foundation*. Epilepsy Foundation, 2010. Web. 8 Dec. 2010.

5. Ibid.

6. Steven C. Schachter. "Who Gets Epilepsy?" *epilepsy. com*. epilepsy.com, 16 Oct., 2006. Web. 8 Dec. 2010.

CHAPTER 2. WHY ME? CAUSES, RISK FACTORS, AND PREVENTION

1. "Epilepsy and Seizure Statistics." *Epilepsy Foundation*. Epilepsy Foundation, 2010. Web. 17 June 2011.

2. "Teens and Sleep." *National Sleep Foundation*. National Sleep Foundation, 2011. Web. 5 Aug. 2011.

CHAPTER 3. SOLVING THE MYSTERY: DIAGNOSIS

1. Stacey Petter. Personal Interview. 9 Jan. 2011.
2. Deivasumathy Muthugovindan and Adam L. Hartman. "Pediatric Epilepsy Syndromes." *The Neurologist* 16 (2010): 223–237. Print.

CHAPTER 4. THE NITTY-GRITTY: TYPES OF SEIZURES

1. Thomas R. Browne and Gregory L. Holmes. *Handbook of Epilepsy, 3rd ed.* Philadelphia: Lippincott Williams & Wilkins, 2004. Print.

CHAPTER 5. MEDICINE AND BEYOND: TREATMENT

1. P. Kwan and M.J. Brodie. "Effectiveness of First Antiepileptic Drug." *Epilepsia.* Wiley Online Library. 42.10 (2001): 1255. PDF.
2. Andrew R.C. Kelso and Hannah R. Cock. "Advances in epilepsy." *British Medical Bulletin* 72 (2005): 135–148. Print.
3. "Medications." *Epilepsy Foundation*. Epilepsy Foundation of America, 2010. Web. 5 Aug. 2011.

SOURCE NOTES CONTINUED

CHAPTER 6. YOUR LIFE: MANAGING EPILEPSY

1. "Getting Personal: The Chanda Gunn Story." *epilepsy. com*. epilepsy.com, 2011. Web. 22 June 2011.
2. "Epilepsy and Genius." *epilepsy.com*. epilepsy.com, 15 Dec. 2006. Web. 22 June 2011.

CHAPTER 7. WHAT WILL HAPPEN NEXT?

1. "2007 Epilepsy Research Benchmarks" *National Institute of Neurological Disorders and Stroke.* n.d. Web. 19 June 2011.

CHAPTER 8. FRIENDS AND FAMILY: DEALING WITH SOCIAL ISSUES

1. "Teen Drivers." *Centers for Disease Control and Prevention*. Centers for Disease Control and Prevention, n.d. Web. 10 Jan. 2011.

CHAPTER 9. HELP! HELPING YOURSELF AND OTHERS

1. "Poverty in the United States Frequently Asked Questions." *National Poverty Center*. National Poverty Center, n.d. Web. 10 Jan. 2011.

2. "Treatment of Migraine Headache in Children and Adolescents." *American Academy of Neurology*. American Academy of Neurology, 2004. Web. 24 July 2011.

3. Amy M. Branum and Susan L. Lukacs. "Food Allergy Among U.S. Children: Trends in Prevalence and Hospitalizations." *Centers for Disease Control and Prevention*. Centers for Disease Control and Prevention, Oct. 2008. Web. 10 Jan. 2011.

4. "Child Maltreatment 2009." *US Department of Health and Human Services, Administration for Children and Families*. US Department of Health and Human Services, Administration for Children and Families, 2010. Web. 10 Jan. 2011.

5. "L. A. Turntable Celebrity, DJ Hapa, Epilepsy Therapy Project Spokesperson Leading Our Team at the National Walk for Epilepsy." *epilepsy.com*. epilepsy.com. 27 Feb. 2007. Web. 17 June 2011.

INDEX

ABOUT THE AUTHOR

Sara Cohen Christopherson is a science writer, educator, and consultant based in Madison, Wisconsin. She writes content for K–12 educational materials and the general public, conducts life science classes and lectures for University of Wisconsin–Madison programs, and provides content expertise for science education program evaluation across the United States. Sara has an undergraduate degree in biology and a master's degree in science education.

PHOTO CREDITS